The Tampering of My Soul

A Book of Intense Poetry, Micro Stories, Journal Entries, and Quotes

Makenzie Decuire R.

authorHOUSE

AuthorHouse™
1663 Liberty Drive
Bloomington, IN 47403
www.authorhouse.com
Phone: 1 (800) 839-8640

Published by AuthorHouse 01/22/2018

ISBN: 978-1-5246-9029-8 (sc)
ISBN: 978-1-5246-9027-4 (hc)
ISBN: 978-1-5246-9028-1 (e)

Library of Congress Control Number: 2017909816

Print information available on the last page.

This book is printed on acid-free paper.

Micro stories are fiction and are not a reflection of the authors personal experiences.

For BJ

Prologue

It's safe to say that writing poetry has and continues to save my life. I see poetry in everything that I do and in everything around me. It is in the smiles and tears of strangers, the weather, the water, the food, our bodies and our creator. Poetry is simply another lens focused on our lives. It is one of our greatest allies under God. Because God reads hearts but poetry are its words.

Growing up I struggled with many things but my temper was the most challenging. I'm not sure if the anger was from being a fatherless child or my stained childhood but my anger became an addiction. My pain was a prison and I longed for a freedom of expression that seemed so unreachable. I hid behind anger because sadness was too vulnerable of an emotion to expose. As I grew older writing poetry, journal entries and stories became my therapy.

I wrote my first poem at the age of eight or nine years old and I distinctively remember showing my mom what I had wrote with pride, she didn't believe that I had written something so "powerful". That was the start of my liberation and fierceness as a writer. I had found my calling in the place where I was hurting the most. My heart.

When I'm writing its work and with any work we do, we need tools. I have five main tools that I work with when writing and these tools are used to keep my poetry tailored to me and my style. The first tool that I use is my womanhood. A reader is to know that I am a woman and that my femininity and womanhood will always play a key part in my experience in the world. The second tool (these are not necessarily in this order) is my blackness. Being black in America is not a mere cultural jacket but an involvement and statement. My reader must feel my fist balled and raised to the sky, they must hear my ancestors screams and songs alike, they must feel the drums, taste the ripeness of histories fruit or the bitterness of its rot. But yes, they must know that I am a black woman! The third tool is pain. There is a message in pain that I use to say to my reader, "I understand and love you". Empathy can be given in abundance when I use pain as a tool. My fourth writing tool is spirituality. I believe in Jehovah God and I feel extremely blessed with my gift to write. I am also very grateful that my moral code has been based on my knowledge of God and his righteous standards. I must say that my spirituality tool is one of the strongest that I have. My last tool is love, and in my opinion love speaks so loudly for itself...

Table of Contents

A lighter shade of black: A plight against colorism

A conspiracy is a very calculating occurrence. In most inner-city neighborhoods, there are pivotal things that will play constituent for its residents (and to their demise). You may notice stores where one can purchase cheap liquor, off-brand grocery establishments that will sell low market goods, uninhabitable houses and apartment buildings that need renovation, the poor, hungry and unheard. However, these are surface and economic structural pains that cause distress; there are many other horrific crimes in minority neighborhoods that affect its people. And for me, colorism was one of them.

Colorism is defined as- Prejudice against individuals with a darker skin tone, typically among the same ethnic or racial group

I grew up in San Francisco Hunter's point Bay view district; this area was mainly populated by African American folk. I realized at a very tender age that my skin color played a part in how I was treated amongst my peers, mainly other blacks. There was an unspoken but distinct division between darker skinned blacks and lighter skin blacks that was undeniable. Elementary school was when I first noticed the difference. I'd have a minor altercation and was quickly called "piss colored" or "white bitch", "conceited" or statements that lead on that I somehow thought I was better. Initially I was perplexed about these cruel remarks because I had never felt separate from the other black students. I just assumed we were all black and all came from the same type of homes and upbringing. But because it was brought to my attention I was forced to try to understand if I was different in some way. That was the first time I ever questioned who I was as a black person.

I had slim interactions with other races including the Samoans and Cambodians that lived in nearby projects because in school the children seem to lean more towards the children who looked like them. There was an implicit familiarity that provided comfort and connection. However, I very much wanted to be friends with them and pretty much was well received after a few tries. Problems arose when I'd try to blend friendships with my black friends and other raced friends. The nonblack kids were not as accepting like they had been for me. I wondered why. What was the difference? Did skin color play a part in how well I was received even though I too was African American? It wasn't long before my curiosity was confirmed. I would get asked questions like, "what are you mixed with?" or "you're so pretty you don't look black". These comments were to assert the stereotypical views that non-blacks had about my race. I was a black girl but not a black girl- an exception. They treated my skin color as a pass into their cultural norms. They couldn't dare attribute my beauty or kindness as a part of my blackness. It had to be subtracted to fit their ideas.

As adulthood approached I had an epiphany that I was privileged in some way by my color, I likened it to an essay that I read about white privilege written by a woman by the name of Peggy McIntosh called "unpacking the invisible Knapsack". McIntosh's thesis gave insight on white privilege and how the knapsack is freely given to whites without cause, the prerequisite is to simply be born white. McIntosh also compared her white privilege to the infamous male privileged in our society. She listed privileges that she can count on cashing in each day, which got me thinking about how my light skin privilege has helped me move about in a white world that a darker skin person couldn't. A few things that came to mind was friendship. I had a higher chance of befriending other raced people because I looked less threatening (with the assumption that darker skinned individuals look more threatening). Another privileged was the mark of beauty- being lighter skinned was closer to the American white standard of beauty. Although these things may seem trivial to some, they have had a significant impact on how lighter blacks move about in their communities and ultimately the world.

I've always felt that I owned a "black card". I strongly believed that I walked into rooms with my blackness first and that my blackness was undeniably noticeable. But did I have a light skin knapsack that I received from birth? If so, could the Willie Lynch letter written back in 1712 be the cause of this unscrupulous behavior? Maybe my Knapsack was a privilege that was made during slavery and maybe I was essentially (yet metaphorically) a House Nigger. I was more palatable to non-blacks when it came to business and friendships even though I wasn't necessarily always relatable. Just the look of me was enough to keep the color lines in the comfortable grey. I dare to say that colorism in my opinion is one of many great conspiracies. So, what shall we do about it?

The African American Experience is intense on many levels and we as a people and culture face horrific asymmetrical treatment. Post slavery intuition black movements had one major component for success which was unity and togetherness. Unity first with our immediate family, unity second with our neighbors and communities, unity third in patronizing minority businesses and positive causes, unity in ideologies and moral standards (even if this area is just respect for moral differences), unity in standing together in times of hardships and most importantly unity in loving our brother. If we are busy uplifting one another and treating one another with the upmost love and respect, there will be no room for colorism. Colorism couldn't survive in a strong bonded atmosphere. And we all become scholars in teaching other raced people how to treat us because how we treat each other becomes the example.

Color has its place, and that is to make the world beautiful... it is art.

And if at any time color becomes tainted with separating one beautiful thing from another, then we shall stay seeing in the grey until we are loving enough to not abuse it.

AMERIKA

Blinded by the dream of equality
A system so corrupt it's contagious
You hear me?

Privileged kids never see the eye of poverty
Churches burn down besieged with mediocrity
Politician's profit we are just numbers and statistics
We sit on death row without confirmation of ballistics
Time is money the beginning and the seed
But how do we prosper if we feed off of greed?

How do we prosper when affection dies
In its creed?

The world is in a hurry running over its neighbors
The American flag sits proudly as a waiver
Many lives stolen -just cargo on boats
Culture stripped bare
Black names die on the coast

Women are murdering their children
PRO CHOICE!

Black faces shunned in the media
NO VOICE!

Amerika Amerika
Let down your blonde hair
A white privilege design
Is obliviousness to despair?

Amerika Amerika you've taken more than you give back
Its agape love you lack
You've infused my community with crack
Now there's an epidemic
Yes there's an epidemic
A calculated pillage
They've intoxicated the village

GentrIfIcatIon
Pushes us deeper in slums
Meatless dinners for our children
Education….. the usage of guns
Diseased generations
And your diseased proclamations
The lynch letters were not just statements
They paved the way for our detested nation
Liberty Oh liberty your poor is dying young
Should you get the death sentence
For lives taken but not won?

Lives taken
But not won.

Breast milk

Mama is partial
She can see no fault in her boy child

Though he is now a man
With sexual escapades and thick facial hair
His testosterone is just a reminder that she bore a man that will
love her without condition
A man that subjects his love without discontentment.... he
becomes her king

He stirs inside her
The construct of what a man means to
Womanhood
Femininity
And womb

His cries are as familiar
As the day, he was born
When needs are met
And wants acknowledged

mama is partial
to that boy of a man

as I sit in the distance
I feel the hurtful independence that was
Engraved inside of me
simply because I too am woman

The ruthlessness of carrying the weight of a husband or father
Snags my throat and kills me

She taught me well

To mend pieces of a foundationless home
To do it alone if need be
To keep my dignity even when famished

now I become my brother's keeper
a traditional legacy of being a daughter
chastised for duplicating her vagina....to one day bare my own

son.

Wedding Band

With this ring, I thee wed
I married a white man
Yup
That's what I said

So now my blackness is crucified
Cause my love has blue eyes
It contradicts my pride
It contradicts my pride?

No that's a fucking lie

At no point do I yearn for his privilege
He's just a man apart of my village
A human being just flesh and bones
I am still a queen from an African home

Black love is any love we give freely
It is not compacted to just one entity
At no point am I prisoned to give my love to a certain man
My love is a gift, my choice, my stance

So, I've decided to give you back your card
To not be pro black since I become your scar
To keep my head high and my crown upright
To know when to be silent and when to put up a fight
To know an opinion holds no real weight
To know that my blackness is not up for debate

Sincerely yours truly the girl who shoots back
I'm no longer pro black
I'm pro mak
I'm pro found
And that's my pro facts

Bj's September

Once upon a time my father bloomed in September, after him I sprouted there too, after me... my son.

My belly swelled to perfection and God deemed him a ripe fruit. My legs were tree branches parted at the center but unstable and green. The coming seed would solidify my womanhood and my avid craving for nurture. Seasons before, my insides were untrustworthy and I had failed and lost a soul without ever hearing his cries. That seed went back to the earth where I conceived him, never to bud again. Nine months ago, I bravely pushed on to serve as an incubator once again- praying to make it once again. On a September morning, the sun came rushing into my room painting everything around me in drastic color. Even though I was in crushing pain nothing mattered more than this legacy. My offspring was making his own season, his own garden in our world. My screams filled the air but my gratitude filled my spirit and with each push bearing down I was brought closer to being renamed .... MOMMY. Bj's September landed on the ninth day in midday hours. He is his father's son, his mother's heartbeat and his family's' heirloom.

Tiny hands

Dear Journal,

Today is an afterthought entry. I haven't had the courage to write about this experience before because of the trauma; however now...I think I'm ready... I think I can do this...

Picture this

My son Bj is playing happily on the floor with his new toy and I'm smiling at his innocent obliviousness. I'm sitting Indian style on the couch, writing and recalling. I swear being a child is the purest moments of our lives. Being a child is so mawkishly beautiful.

When I decided to finally publish my poetry something vivid stirred in me, this book would complete my life before I die. So, in that moment I made peace with myself and released all my complexities on paper. My hope is to touch another "Makenzie" out there in the world. I'll share a story with you about how motherhood betrayed and blessed me and how it gave me courage for other facets of my life.

If memory serves me correctly, sometime in 2010 my "baby fever" was at an all-time high. I realized five years before, that I was not fertile. I had not been a virgin since I was sixteen and rarely took birth control. My boyfriend and I met when I was nineteen and were like many other young couples (having sex often) not using protection and being irresponsible. However, after five years I had never fell pregnant (although I wasn't necessarily trying). My cycle had been irregular all my life and I questioned if it played a part in my infertility. I began doing heavy research for about a year on my symptoms. I came across information about a condition called "polycystic Ovarian Syndrome" and made a doctor appointment to confirm what I believed to be the culprit. I was correct; the obgyn

11

found many tiny cysts on both of my ovaries. I was devastated. At the time I was overweight, constantly depressed and I concluded that I was barren.

Meanwhile, most of my girlfriends and family members were welcoming beautiful healthy babies into the world. I had never felt so partial in my life. I thought it would be unbearable to never know what motherhood was like. I just couldn't live with myself.

I found peace in being Proactive. I got on a low carbohydrate diet and lost forty pounds in six weeks. I went from a size eleven to a size three. I got acupuncture and took Chinese herbs. I was super excited about the possibility of conceiving. A good friend of mine introduced me to a book called "the secret" and how powerful words are when speaking positive thoughts into the universe. I fantasized about how my baby would feel inside of my belly, and how he/she would look. Those wonderful thoughts consumed me. When I look back now in retrospect, I believe part of my yearning was just to see myself as something greater than I was. I had always admired the unique relationships that mothers had with their children. I wanted to be loved in that way and love another person in that way. It was a society of special feelings that I felt like I deserved, mainly because I am a woman.

In June 2011, I took a pregnancy test around four am while in the mode of getting ready for work. I had taken so many tests in the past I had gotten use to the "negative" results but not today my pregnancy test was positive! I began thanking Jehovah in prayer. Thank you, God! Thank you for this blessing! I instantaneously went into mommy mode; this tiny being was depending on me. I immediately woke Brian "Guess what?"

Sometime in October during a prenatal visit I mentioned to my doctor a concern of mine. I explained to her that my baby felt low and as the baby got bigger I felt weird pains that didn't seem normal. I also spotted the first six weeks of my first trimester (which was very scary for me). She was nonchalant about my concerns and *after quickly checking my cervix she dryly says, "You're fine". I thought to myself eh maybe I am being a bit paranoid.*

On November 10, 2011 (approx.20 weeks gestation) I was working my normal shift (which meant I was standing all day serving food to customers) I'd been feeling extremely tired the entire morning. I was bloated and I had been to the restroom numerous of times trying to have a bowel movement. I just assumed that I had some type of weird pregnancy constipation. Unbeknownst to me at the time, the uncomfortable pressure and tingling in my groin were contractions.

I got home and called my mom. I described the pain and the uncontrollable urge to have a bowel movement, she told me it was normal, just pains of a growing baby. I then called Brian (my boyfriend) he pretty much said the same thing. A few hours later the urge became more intense and I was back on the toilette trying to relieve myself of the pressure. My body began pushing on its own. It was so devastatingly natural. After pushing and pushing I felt something inside of my vagina. I swear my heart stopped beating. I touched the opening and felt a slick ball inside. I nervously took a mirror to see what it was. Is it my baby? Oh God what have I done? The mirrors reflection showed a grey looking sack that I feverishly pushed back inside of me. I called Brian in hysterics "Take me to the emergency room now- something is wrong with the baby!!!"

In the E.R on the table an immediate ultrasound was done. I could see my baby swimming around content and free. A normal heart beat, normal growth, he was fine and watching him made me feel hopeful. But I had dilated two centimeters and the sack had completely descended into my vagina. The risk of infection was too great for an intervention. I looked at the doctor with tears streaming down my face and asked frankly, "will my baby be ok?" he shook his head, "I'm sorry, you're going to be admitted to labor and delivery, there isn't much we can do".

I prayed out loud" please God help me I can't lose my baby! Please God let my baby live" In that moment I became numb and a weird calmness came over me that was filled with disbelief and pain. I had died on that table. I was in active pre-term labor. My baby wasn't going to make it.

Brian Alexander Russell Jr. was born "sleeping" November 11th, 2011 at 6:45 am.

He wasn't quite a pound. He had tiny blonde hairs all over his face. I kissed his ten tiny toes and ten tiny fingers. He was perfect to me. As I held my son I found solace in being his mom. I didn't realize I wouldn't be taking him home, my mind wouldn't allow me to understand anything other than my natural role as his mother.

Leaving the hospital was an outer body experience. They wheeled me out past rooms filled with new born baby cries. At one point, I believed that I was leaving the hospital to get back home to my pregnancy. It was as if I was leaving the nightmare with Kaiser and somehow going home would make things the way they were. I left the hospital with a breast full of milk and discharge papers that read:

Miscarriage at 19.5 weeks Gestation
Gender- Boy
Weight- 285 grams
Diagnosis-Incompetent cervix
Further instructions-Patient must have cerclage for subsequent pregnancies
No intercourse for six weeks

On paper, I was just another woman who had a miscarriage. I was just another woman who would have to try again. I felt the silent insufficient pity from some of the nurses. I also felt the coldness of one nurse who casually sat my deceased baby on a bed side table while she wrote notes on a chart. To the medical staff, my child was just another unfortunate circumstance but for me he was all I had. I was left feeling recklessly empty.

When I returned home, everything looked foreign. My bedroom where I conceived, my kitchen where I cooked meals, my bathroom where I had vomited because of morning sickness- all seemed like a different space. I felt like a guest who needed to get acquainted with the living quarters. Is it true? Am I home without my baby? Am I that girl? How do I explain this? Who am I, now that I'm no longer a mother? I was lifeless. The mourning turned into a bottomless depression that made me peculiar and introverted. I shut myself off from the world for almost two years.

When I finally returned to work I found it difficult to help pregnant customers. While watching tv I always changed the channel when diaper commercials came on. I never walked down the baby isle in stores either. Anytime I heard of a new pregnancy in my family I would cry myself to sleep. It was a pain that kept on hurting. I was just a shell of a woman and looking back now I don't know how I got through it. I have done a pretty good job of suppressing until now. Now that I am writing and sharing my story I'm forced to face the loss. Sharing this with you dear reader is my way of healing and it is in the core of my writing.

The most incredible hopeless feeling in the world is not being able to protect your child. I couldn't protect my unborn son from the inadequacy of my womb. I allowed guilt to make maggots out of my heart. I had to wake up and love the baby that once lived inside of me but accept that he was gone and I'd have to try again. I was still a mother but now a mother in mourning. And I had to be ok with that. To just be …ok.

I conceived for the second time January 2014. BJ (Brian Alexander Russell Jr.) was named after his brother. He was born September 9, 2014 weighing seven pounds four ounces. He is our blessing, perfect and gorgeous. I have never known love to this magnitude before.

The Prototype of Ghetto

We stamp this hapless label
On pretty dark
Faces
Instead of saying nigger
To segregate the races
… In social situations

Who is, where is, what is Ghetto?

Is it some god forsaking place?
The metropolitan degree
Full of tenuous minorities
Can you see the ghetto in me?
Can you see it in me?

Yea you see it in me…

Is ghetto a homemade language?
An unacceptable parlance
You're saying; excuse me I do not understand
She uneducated, she has no stance
She has no stance

We fight the power with the power that's given
They put us in ghettos as a way of black living
Then we submerge trying to stay alive
But wealth was not designed for blacks with pride

Who is, what is, where is ghetto?

A Mentality
Maybe
Like when Brenda threw out her baby
Or when Rodney King got beat and went crazy
Or the dream that was stolen from king from our youth
Or how nobody understands the words of Badu
Bob Marley once told us we are buffalo soldiers
And as the ghetto makes us colder
The real world sits on our shoulders…

But who is, where is, what is ghetto?

Please refrain
My mother gave me a name

Ghetto is many things
A place and an attitude, but worst of all
A jacket
Thrown on people out of simple habit
A world that is not accepting because it is neglecting
Let's start by respecting

Let the word die
And start correcting

No one, nothing and no where
Should be ghetto
Because there is enough of everything for your brother
Humanity needs each other
And it all starts
With structure

CIGS

You've made me a servant to your poison
Now I rely on the hard fix
Crushing my fragile lungs
To become cancerous
And die

I look for you after great sex
A perfect mix of cum and smoke
To end a beautiful night
Of fornication

Hand and hand they perish together

I look for you when my cup is full
Speaking in conversations soon
Forgotten

I search for you while my nose
French kisses cocaine
Watching the clock run away
With my rotting conscience

An empty box lay next to an empty straw
A table
A chair
A pack

I keep looking because I am an addict
But even more so a creature of habit
Rituals and consistencies we have no theory over
So in my findings I've come to know myself behind the cloud of
smoke
Yes
I am your runaway slave
The one who got away
And the one
Who

Quit

Bj

If someone took a scalpel
To my chest
And cut me
There he would sit...
With eyes that mimic mine
And lips
Like my father
Hair
As potent as the sunrise
A marvelous creature

Love in this respect
Struggles to define what I feel
The soul of this child
Is my breathing

Air

I'd suffocate
Without him

Oh Jehovah
How well you have done
Blessing me with this responsibility
A
Son

My sweet Alexander

You are
Nothing short
Of
My
Universe …

Hot glass

He prefers a glass pipe
Over my devotion

I search for his calls
After ten pm

I'd like to slice his throat for keeping me
In pain

But who would plan the funeral?

He is friendless
No sharing secrets

Borrowed demons making them his own

There is nothing to live for when he drives away
Nothing to die for because he is dead

I melt in my blankets covered by sadness
Insomnia prisons me, utterly lonely

He doesn't deserve me
We live on co dependency
Both of us sickly
Disturbed
Unhealthy

He prefers a glass pipe
Over my devotion

I search for his calls after ten pm

I'd like to slice his throat for keeping me
In pain

Then I can begrudgingly
Plan
His funeral

Jewerly Box

Undignified and fearless
Mutates into avidity
And pain
Because I found my flower
While holding a bouquet

They asked me why reach for the sky
While having the stars?
Because I yearn to have the galaxy in my palms
Massaging it as it purrs

So I left the ring on the dresser
Placed it in a pretty jewelry box
It began screaming out to me
As I put on lace stockings
Stilettos
Lipstick
It kept reading scriptures
And quoting my conscious
Asking me to stay home

But without a glance
Behind me
I held tightly to the rose
That had been picked out of ungratefulness
The rose was still tender
Only because it was plucked by me

Full fingers
A girl that has felt the world
Climax in her bosom

Now whos to say she is
Still pure
When none of her petals
Are admired
By morning

Leaving

Shouldn't we break free from freedom?
Confine ourselves to each other
With the shunning of this world
With us- is what we have lukewarm
Spitting us out with our covert insecurities

Though
You have embodied
The innocent unknowing
I feverishly make mistakes in our behalf
Self pity sits with my guilt
Literally....killing me

I know men have conversations
Foreign to women's ears
But in the moments of betrayal
They speak invisibly to the universe
Bringing into existence
A woman scorned

Yes we should break free from freedom
Release ourselves to ourselves
While embracing this curious world
And
If I drive away
Leaving dust in your eyes
And the letters of my plates waving to our memories
I have not failed you
Failed us
Failed love
Maybe I have offered
The definition of what love is in this moment
So

We
Live
It

Nigga

We use this word in some conversations
To speak of our husbands enticing provocations
A greeting to some -we say it's endearing
How frivolous and shameful our forefathers were fearing
Did we somehow forget what this horrid word means?
Do we hide those secrets like the strange fruit on strange trees?

A pitchfork to our blackness obliteration to the psyche
Chattel to the master, a piece of disposable property

How ironic we use the same tools to destroy our building
Branding ourselves
Branding our children
Hot branding tool for a runaway stock
The letter eats the skin and the soul dries out to rot

We use this word easily like a devil in deciet
Haunting one another, smothering ourselves in their sheets
Cotton picking, blister having, sweaty little slave
Where the tobacco grows is a hallow hole for a grave

We keep speaking our darkness to the sour pits of hell
We keep losing our heritage to the gruesomeness of its spell
It cuts, it cringes, it spoils and it kills us
It breaches air to thrill us, so we never become the real us

We use this word in some conversations
To speak of our husbands enticing provocations
We should learn the proper way to greet our brother
Counteract the transgression not give birth to another
Crowns misplaced, gold stolen from the land
Bandages and bondage in pale white sands
But
Let us keep going with our kinky locks to the sky
Singing songs of praise for release
Letting the dreadful word
Die.

Purging

He sat out on a journey
With uneven pavement
Rocks and gravel crunching sadly
In his socks
The moon is yellow but full
As he howls
In search of ecstasy

He is no longer romantic
Or human
Or mine

Baby came screaming with
Rainbow eyes
We loved each other to love him
But love was contested as the gravel and rocks
Lay closely by the door
Asking him to come home
Be with us
You love us

So I detoxed his broken bones
In my yard
His bloody tissues in my bathroom,
His crooked smile, bitter laughter,
His clothes, his shoes
His heart

I purged a man with muscle and muse, triumph
And failure, spark and ash

He was purged so that I could clean my own closet
Find something nice to wear
Even if dinner is served
For one.

Reservations

You reserve your thoughts
Why prevent our closeness?
My hands are open
I offer them to you
I say to you calmly with an uncommon coaxing
Reveal yourself to me
I will not hurt you

You reserve your intentions and keep me at bay
I tongue your ego with no discretion
I cannot pretend I am unmoved by you
Reveal yourself to me
I will not hurt you

You reserve you intimacy because you believe I'm ravenous
Then smile at how easily
Sexiness comes to me
I am not pretentious
I am persistent
Reveal yourself to me
I will not hurt you

Or maybe I will
When we disagree on small things
When you need my attention
When walls are up with no strings
When the night gets chilly and my blanket isn't warm
When you're tired and have no strength to weather the storm
Or maybe in moments I can't look you in the eye
Or the times there's no time and were living separate lives

You reserve your heart and push me away
I am not the lover who cursed you
I am not the lover who cursed you
Although I hold strong, I cannot hold long

Reveal yourself to me
I will not hurt you...

African

Somewhere between my skin complexion
And the
Brown eyes
I wear for my own direction
You hate me close
For its your perception

I'm African I'm African
yes, sir I am

This world spills over with lies and deceit
Dogma and propaganda
From the Powers that be

Another

Black

Face

You'd hate to meet...

Our children are in havoc from this doom
No mercy for our offspring they die too soon
women take on roles men should hold in a home
A teenage girl sits pregnant and alone

But this not us to our bone

This is not us to our core

Greatness was stolen and brought a shore

It's weird how they stare then turn and look away
We care what they think but they're blind in what they say

Stereotypical, uptight
Critical
So, we hold to our spiritual
The only light that kept us
Livable

Mother nature failed in her wonderous plan
Leaving her legacy in the harshest of hands
They offer the food when we're too exhausted to eat
Our bodies weary, tired, no sleep

But who am I
Little bitty me
Just a very tiny part
Of an entire entity

Somehow, we are hampered by our skin complexion

The brown Eyes

We wear for our own direction
They hate
Us
Close

For its their perception
We are Africans We are Africans

Yes, sir we are
We are Africans We are Africans

Yes sir we are...

I LET A WHITE MAN LOVE ME

I guess I can't raise my fist with the best of em
I can't rally or riot or be pro for my people
If I'm not anti white then I'm anti black
And if I let him love me
It's the black that he lacks

I guess them crackas are all up to no good
Not to be trusted and evil to the bone
Their white sheets lay close on beside tables
Girl you better leave that white man alone

Your husband looks mixed they ask- is he Creole?
Where that hair come from it aint nappy enough
Why he talk like that he aint strappy enough
He aint dark like us he aint Negro enough

I let that white man love me take me all the way under
I let that man get close put my blackness asunder

Put my blackness asunder

Please
I will raise my fist high cause my roots are in the Congo
I will rally and riot with my kinky blonde afro
And if he loves me in my skin cause he's drunk of m-e-l-a-n-I-n
I'll let him sip this Ghana gin cause my Africa is not a sin

I let a man love me in his own feverish right
And he stepped into my darkness
Because he wasn't afraid
Of my light

He wasn't afraid

of my light

A different type of freedom

Women jail their forbidden bodies to suppress sexuality
Eroticism is only supposed to be seen or acknowledged in the
construct of a marriage... It's in the bible

Young women are being circumcised somewhere in the world
so they do not feel the pleasure of a penis
The beautiful penis is not just to make drawers pissy right?

Is it wrong to allow your lady-part to become a renegade and
leave a trail of orgasms behind?

I'd like for men to salivate over just the thought of me, because
for once in my life I'd like to define myself strictly from the angle
of my sexuality
taking Freedom... FREEDOM leaking from the seams of my
undergarments
FREEDOM dripping from the deepness of my walls
FREEDOM that shames the mother who tells you to wear your
dress below the knee, to never show cleavage and to watch how
fitting your clothes are

FREEDOM to express and explore your own body
FREEDOM to be safe in our exploration
 And the FREEDOM to not be raped or judged on our journey

 FREEDOM to be a lover and loved on
That kind of FREEDOM is longed for by the homemaker
The professional
The young woman
The older woman
The disabled woman

The single woman
The taken woman
The religious woman
The colorless woman
The colorful woman
The artistic
The sadistic
The visionary
The doctor
The scientist

Yes, we women are in every genre of life... and we too want the freedom
To be alive in our hearts
even if sometimes beats

In our lingerie...

There are predators in our world seeking to devour and ruin our children. They are members of our churches, members of our school systems, neighbors, acquaintances and members of our families.

"The virgin with no heart beat" is a fiction micro story about a young girl who falls victim to a predator in her family. This story is a small yet powerful dedication to all the innocent vulnerable souls who've went through similar accounts.

This story is for all of you who's voices have been silenced.

We are ready to hear your stories, we are ready to help you heal. We love you.

The virgin with no heartbeat

A red circle big enough for the bulk of my forehead burned in his mind essentially making me his target. I could feel the irony in his revolting and his addictions made him bizarre and uncanny. Momma loved him, so she took his hand in marriage and gifted me with my own personal holocaust that changed my beginnings forever. My siblings too young to understand or save me gave me a unique fear that maybe their fates could duplicate mine. I had been punished for taking too long for making sandwiches, forgetting to dispose of the trash, wearing pink lip gloss, sweeping and summoning dust. But was I being punished for money lost at a gambling shack, bad dope, memories that haunted, broken relationships, deaths, hopelessness and unparalleled rage? His eyes were daunting and disturbing as they examined my flesh with urgency. I was whisked away closer to him than comfortable and didn't dare scream. His sweaty hands were callused and more destructive than I could remember; my memories were only of seeing his hands place candles on a birthday cake, or his hands under a hood to fix our family car, or his hands wiping my snotty nose when sick, or hands modified to be gentle... to not hurt me. But today his hands are hostile with thievery and malediction and as he entered in to my virginity I cried out to God and became a non-believer. I could no longer hear my heart beating, I could no longer taste the Sunday dinners cooked, or the way grass smelled when wet in summer. With every pump, with every kiss, I kept dying and erasing memories that once bonded making us a unit. He put flames to anything that resembled love and all that was left was detestation for his presence and the cutting eyes of my scorned mother.

Black Man

I've looked at this man
This is my observation
My black man is not common
He is my beginning
My foundation
He is lost at times
And I realize
It is difficult for he
But my backbone is strong
He is the best part of me
African cannot describe
What I see when I look into his face
Gutters and ghettos give no justice
To his powerful demeanor of race

And it's sad to see
What we see in this day
How these men are afraid
Of what's locked deep away
No one can judge him
He has potential to change
But he has short respect
Because they stole his real name

We influence ourselves
When we leave behind morals
We kill off our dreams
Because of our sorrows
And the beauty you lose is
Too thick to let go
But the most important value
Is the small beauty you know
It's hard to see a mirror and know
That's your face
It's even harder to understand the place you sit
Is your space
But how do we grow
If we don't see any bigger
What to do you stand for when you call your brother
Nigger
How can you communicate if you can't speak or spell
What can you offer when you're trapped in a cell
Success takes a toll on those minds that will swell
And you leave behind your women
Too cocky to prevail

I cook and clean
I rub your back and kiss your black lips
I wash all your clothes
You still have nerve to say
Bitch
You laugh at my hair
It's too kinky you say
You wallow in a shadow
You will die in that way
That mentality so erratically has no peace or a treaty
I share you not to dare you
Even though my hearts greedy

You are almost mist without me
But with me you are a whole
So to be with me in harmony
Is like the riches of African gold

I am the black woman
I am she
I will stand
But my essence will have no meaning
If we don't cure
The true
Black
Man

Daily Simplicity

Self affirmations
And reminder notes on mirrors
To pray

Kitchen swollen with dishes
And bedroom hurricaned by laundry

Ugh where is the time?

I dust off my bible
And open to a random verse

Immediately I remember to not be anxious over
This day or tomorrow
For each day will have anxieties of its own

I cook eggs in an old pot
And turn on the news

My baby is smiling reaching for me

Suddenly
I feel warm

Because happiness
Can be
So
Simple

Black Girl

Black girl you know this life aint fair
When beauty means bleaching skin
And wearing Asian hair…

While sitting in front of the television taking braid extensions out of my hair, a Pantene shampoo commercial comes on. The white woman in the commercial has thick, dark- brown hair that flows past her shoulders: a lion's mane. Her hair gave her a certain-type attractiveness and femininity that I hadn't seen or felt while wearing my own natural hair. Was it the length or texture? As I stared I realized that her face was mundane, but her hair gave her a societal stamp of approval that some weird part of me yearned for. And this hair was attainable from purchasing a five-dollar shampoo?! You gota be kidding me.

Black girl this life doesn't have to hurt you
Find your virtues
Find your virtues

If at any time you need to be reminded that you are black- run your fingers through your kinky hair. In my community, this is called Nappy hair- not the "good" curly stuff that mixed girls and some fortunate non-mixed girls have. Nappy hair is the hair that some of us hide from the world because our insecurities are deeper than our pride. A lot of little black girls are taught early on by their peers and the world that we do not meet beauty's requirements. We understand the message when we are shopping for Barbie's and baby dolls but can only pick from white dolls with long blonde hair. We understand the message when we are forced to get our hair straightened (either with heat or a perm) for it to be more manageable but also to be more accepted. The heat and the chemicals ultimately ruin the natural state of African American hair. The hair breaks from chemical damage and some become bald from traction alopecia. We carry the shame of our hair and treat it as a scar all the while becoming huge consumers to the hair business. The hope is to grow our hair long or give the illusion that our texture is straight or wavy. We prove time and time again that we are our biggest hair critics. Essentially, believing European beauty is standard. It is the biggest lie some of us black girls believe.

Black girl you know this life a sin
When they make you shame your black hair and skin?
How can you live with the pain within?

A black woman by the name of Christina Jenkins Patented the process of hair weaving back in the fifties. The oldest known wig wearers date back to the Egyptian times. Even in Ancient Greece and Rome kings and Queens both wore wigs for esthetic reasons and to not appear as weak leaders. So, for centuries hair has been of huge importance, grace and stature. Even the bible says that hair is a woman's glory. We women of all colors feel the greatness in hair, right? However black women are suffering in a unique way when it comes to hair... why?

Black girl this life doesn't have to hurt you
Find your virtues
Find your virtues

In 1966 The black panther party formed and was a huge part of the civil rights movement. The AFRO was a part of showing strength, power, resilience and unwavering beauty. The Afro is the black hair in its natural state. It comes in different textures of kink, varied sizes, thickness and color but each Afro is beautiful and bold just the same. Uncovering our beauty and revealing it to the world in a bold way forced others to acknowledge our uniqueness and accept us in how God created us. The Afro is Poetry.

Black girl you are the first woman created
Your beauty divine
Your hair
An understatement
And in time you will see
And believe
That your hair gives fruit
like

Eden trees...

Willingness

The sad part about love is
The heart is left unprotected
The sensitive organ
Sits alone in a chest
Waiting to be touched by
Unfamiliar hands

You see with love
There's no guarantee
There's no for sure

Yes it's a gamble
Anytime you are brave enough
To lock eyes with a pretty stranger

The sad part about love is
I found the audacity to love you
But my love is beat up
Banged around
Sickly and weak
And now it's bloody in my hands
As I still pose the offer
Asking you sweetly
To still try
To put aside your trepidation
And touch my shattered pieces
Of
Love

Satisfy

While searching for satisfaction
We climb mountains too high for fingertips
And eat shit for nourishment
Because soul searching ain't never been for the faint hearted
Or the timid
Love is tailored to individuals
Yours not like mine
So we meet and shake hands in the middle
Pops didn't show me attention
So I've sucked my way through vineyards of men
Grabbing hold of my arms to prison me
With intimacy
Satan dwells in Dicks not Richards
You understand me?
That's why little girls submit to daddy
As grown women
And we are all looking as time beats us with blackened eyes
Ike Turnering our bodies with age but still searching
Bold and blind
And truth is thrown to dogs because searching for satisfaction
ain't never been sweet
Ain't never tasted like warm butter on cooked bread
No cold water for cactus
And rather we live and die with glasses for armor
Magnifying our desires to claim these desires as our own
There will always be a bit of sorrow stored in our spirits
A map leading
To
No where

Searching for daddy

A man will leave home
And taint his children
Leaving wanting spirits behind
To fend for themselves
In a world full of demons
And sometimes
The prospect
Of intimacy

A girl child will eagerly ache for daddy
Her vagina used as a tool
To gain power in the journey of affection

How often do we see ourselves
In our fathers image
And fall confused
Because daddy is a stranger
With no face
Daddy doesn't know me
So I search for daddy
In
You

Under a spell only men can concoct
A woman's desires are mixed in the potion
And the struggle to be loved and moved by love
Is given away easily
With
Her
Virginity

Flower Shop

Dainty little orchid with roots plumped in the air, her pussy gives off moisture that circles and engulfs.

She needs little water but much attention, as she presses her petals conceitedly to the sky, sucking in the sun and its big ol rays. Her florist is unusually masculine, his business an inheritance, and though his temper is quick his secret affection for the gentle gems are high. He can smell her as he comes in to cut and trim her sisters for profit. She has summoned a visitor that embodied her in human form. A sultry woman with pride and beauty. She too-An orchid. She makes light of a burly man in a flower shop as teeth are shown, names are exchanged and talk of libations on the horizon. Soon, A night with few stars and nippy breezes blow the two to the shop at ungodly hours. Dainty is sitting in a tea room where she can hear kisses. The kisses become prominent and the pair is in the room, close, exposed and pressing against her petals. Petals fall defenselessly to the floor, crying out for devotion. But Florist is consumed by a flower that he had not grown or fostered but making dainty a sacrifice. As she dies she thinks of how the doorbell jingles when visitors come to purchase her sisters, she thinks of how the warmth of the windowsill feels curling around her breast and stems, or how she is the reason women flock to florist because it is her beauty that calls them to him. Swiftly the pressure of their bodies is relieved. She can hear florist speak softly in disappointment as he peers into her petal less body. Her beauty whisked away in seconds, gone. He had traded one flower for another. Killing her soil, never to grow again.

I EVE

You were created sophisticatedly
Your rib took a bruise for me
Your heel did also

But you were intrigued
By sin
So
I fed you the fruit

The juice dripped from your lips
To our calamity
Making cookie cutter imperfection for our
Children

Now I endure laborious pains
And yes I deserve them

But I have not forgotten
That
I am
Your
Initial weakness

HANG ME

I've dug up a notion
A small calamity
My insides reveal
Love is a disadvantage to me
I may give him all I have in my hands
Lying to myself to feel strong
Grabbing on to the fact that I'm truly afraid
To stand in the cold

Alone

The rope is thick
And heavy in weight
One touch of the weapon
I contemplate on my fate
It is wrapped around my neck
I breathe as it's tied
Impatiently waiting for the chair and I
To
Divide
As soon as we kiss
I drop from my stand
An invisible rose petal
Has slipped from his hands

The Illusion

We don't fall
In love

We tippy toe around it
We frolic in its poppies
And sit quietly in its rainbows

We don't fall

In love

We touch its soft mane
We gaze into its rays
Kissing promises into its promises

And if at anytime
Our gait gives way
And we began falling
It is not love that we fall into
But the bitter assumption
That it
Was there.

Men Thieves

I can't let no man steal these kisses
Lord knows they sweet as blueberry pie
I can't let no mister
Grab these thighs
Pull me too close
Break my ties

No sir
No sir

I love me too heavy
To let you in uninvited
Aint no rock
Aint no steady

Because I got me a somebody
Who love on me thick
He adores my glitzy freckles
The softness of my lips

Yes I am every bit of woman
From my feet to my head
You heard what I said?
From my feet to my head!

Go ahead and cut your eyes
I got to be bold
Because love aint for sale

And neither is my soul
And neither is my soul

MY DESIGN

Let your fingers tangle
In my hair
Let your tongue explore
The sweetness of my flower
Let your belly
Say hello to my food
As I cook in heels
And

Nothing else

Let your thoughts go free
As we pillow talk
Bare footed and high ………. On one another
Watch me recite Langston Hughes
Watch me sing Bobby Blue Bland blues

Lovers and fools are the same type of people
I promise it takes courage to choose
Mental stimulation -body manipulation

Designed

Especially

For you

I was designed
Especially
For you

Panties

Because I'm a Woman
Am I a victim to my sex appeal
Am I in submission to my femininity
Some sort of mockery
To my womb

Because I am a woman
Must beauty always take precedence
Over my thoughtful inclinations
Shall it Posses me for the eyes sake
Is there a punishment of pretty's obligation

Do I have to wear panties
Because it's proper
Or sit quietly during conversations
Because I didn't hear my name

Oh yes I am all woman
And girl
And lady
But only in my own right

Because

I said
so

Milk Man

The empty milk jugs sat in front like a vase full of tulips begging for intimacy and her neediness solidly attached. He was late. The screeching sound of tires, high heels clacking and burning obscenities took stage, and suddenly the door became a punching bag. Her youngest accompanied her to the door – with eyes and lips like his father. The screaming woman saw familiarity in the child; she had loved this face with decades in mind. But what did the widow owe, Money for milk or an explanation? Should the widow stay up most nights vigorously cleaning, slumbering in an empty bed salivating for man honey? Should she apologize for quenching her thirst because he wore a band? She accepted the harsh slap as her jealousy left her bosom and dripped down her front steps. She muttered quickly "I understand" although she was not sorry because she was too occupied mourning her lover, her last night when he came inside of her and said "I love you". As she wiped the spit from her blushed cheeks she told herself a secret...I am a hopeless Jezebel.

Artist Amnesty

Poetry aint for no surface dwellers baby
It aint for the people who ignore the pink
In sunsets
Or the sounds humming birds make
After suckling nectar

Poetry aint for the man with voracity
In his eyes
Wanting eyes
His penis making most decisions

Poetry aint for green lives
Youngstas and fools
Those wet behind the ears
Never known enough to be enough for nobody

No way Jose
No way No how

Poetry is an incision
The beautiful infliction spilling out the tender juices
Of the soul

I know this love too well to not share it like fruit
Giving it freely in
Some sort of
Lusty
Abundance

Last call

Love
Didn't see her crying in the shower
Or putting on makeup
Late
In the evening
Squeezing in dresses
That couldn't fit

Love
Didn't see her drowning in
Perfume
Or rehearsing her smile
In foggy mirrors

Love
Was not keen
To her sloppy desperation
Or nail bites
Waiting for Mr.hello

Or the bartender saying
Its
Time
To
Go

The Bruising

We neither come nor go
Without being distressed
By our world

Without at some point
Claiming a fragmented
Heart
Or owning some sort of
Misfortune

We are all specs of dust
Defective beings
Taking advantage
Of the breath of life

And because the prospect
Of happiness
Remains in the distance for our taking
We cling to the possibility
As if it's all we have

And it is

So let's keep speaking candidly
To the universe
Until we have enough courage
To converse
With
God

Unexpected Funeral

Last night
Something died in me
It curled itself into a ball
Whimpering
In sadness
Then closed its eyes
And
Died

I mourned
And
I bled
Cutting your name into my wrist
I buried it in a pretty casket

Last night
Some part of you
Died
In me

Leaving nothing behind
But bones
And
Dust

Fairness

Unfair to many my birth took place
Unfair to the earth

The human race

Mother don't leave me here to die
Mother don't cry
When I live my own life

Father don't leave me here without your lead
Father believe
It's you who bleeds

Brother don't taunt me with stupidity
Brother be weary
Brother please hear me

Sister grow strong into what's inside
Sister my young one
Sister my pride

Jehovah I am helpless
Without your hand to guide me
I am cold without your wisdom
I need your love to recognize me

Unfair to many my birth took place
Still I am here

Holding the tiniest
Space...

Skin

uninhibited
Skin
Touched by unclean hands
His fornication excused by imperfection

He'd turn his back on freedom in a new world
To have compassion
By a companion
Though she does not kneel to your God
Or give thanks to your creator
She still listens to your petitions
And offer her love box
And it's enough
Her tiny love
Is
Enough

Why?

Who can ever know the depth of a woman's
foreign heart
Who can know this?

And
Who can know
 that shadowy places are homes
for those who make Jehovah
a stranger

for the illusion
of love

Imperfection

Decades
Turn teeth into wood
As distant memoirs
We die in old age
As soon as we learn
To live

Babies become adults
And sometimes we outlive them
Lullaby's are soon forgotten
And a mother's voice is recalled at her repass

We are people in history
Forgotten
Or called to mind when stories are told to break myth
Or bring to reason

Because we disintegrate
The moment our cries are heard
 being
Pushed
From
The
Threshold
Of the womb

Quotes & Short Poems

Some of the most horrific crimes are concealed in poverty
Murder does not always mean the death of another person
it sometime means the death of an optimistic spirit
the death of innocence
the death of a dream...

When we climb mountains
It is not the view at the top that makes us tiny
But the sound of our own voice echoing
That humbles us...

My son
you must not be like your father to carry a legacy
You must be much stronger than him
To carry it well
and make it your own...

My love
I only have eyes for you
Even when I'm old and blind
I'll be French kissing our memories
Smiling at the sun...

KISSABLE

Kiss me
So I can write poems to my libido
Swaying these hips like a street woman full of liquor
Kiss me
So my girlfriends talk behind my back
Jealous enough to hurt somebody
Kiss me baby
So I can brag about how you love me
And how soft your lips feel entwined with mine

My goodness
How exceptional
A
Tongue
Can be

Dancing

Tears and rum
Creating some type of cocktail
While the blues rock my bedroom walls

I know damn well he's singing to me
And with me

As I chicken scratch my name
In an Alice Walker book
I'm reminded of how
Simple life use to be
And how easy it was
To
Feel you

9/21/82

At the end of the world
Waiting for me is
September
Aging me for the last time
As a reminder
That I am as ridiculous as my perfect immaturity

Yes my dear September
I have become your bitch
Now I sit having esoteric talk with her
And the wall
Carving my name
On its paint

Just another day
To
Die

Eight am

If the morning had not come
To remind us of last night
We would still have wine on our whispers
And wet kisses on our intimate parts
But
The candles
Have died
And Luther
Has stopped singing
My lipstick is smudged and I cannot find
My panties

Where in the hell does the night go
When the sun
Doesn't love you?

Lust

He took a dance with the devil
And paid well
For my red dress
And it fit like a glove
Against my milky skin.....and transgression
laid its hands under my garments
Searching to consume all parts of me

Could it be?
That I have become his addiction
Inflicting some sort of wanted pain
Dripping
From
His
Ego...

Let us pray

Hands together
Head down
Knees to the floor
Speaking in a tone
Only you
And God can hear

A heart screaming
For mercy

For a new world

Telling our flesh to keep
Quiet

We

Are
Dying

Quotes

Darkness is temporary, even a lie must come from it and reveal itself.

Your will to do great things are wrapped around your persistence; there is no satisfying destiny that has lacked devotion.

A man can stand alone with the willingness to fight, but cannot survive alone with the willingness to love.

Humble yourself because you hold a dangerous tongue, words can be more powerful than the thoughts behind them.

Let us take chances without losing morals, there is no reward for a man with a guilty conscience.

The world is yours for the taking unless you don't believe so, give yourself a reason to conquer and you shall.

The heart is not always trustworthy but it is courageous, so we break our own hearts because we are brave enough to be stupid.

If you are uncomfortable in your own skin, others will be uncomfortable with you wearing it.

Make peace with time so you never grow impatient; make peace with your heart so you never go without being loved.

PRIDE- the one thing we love to have with minimal qualifications.

There are enough resources to take care of the world but the minds of the people must believe it so, greed and selfishness deprives us all.

The beautiful part about light is:
It can shine anywhere
Through anyone
At anytime

Secrets become demons
Demon's multiply
And there is nothing left afterward
But lava
To eat your soul

Pane

Windows beg for eyes
To peer through them

The sun will yearn
For the sky to serve as a canvas
While the brightness wraps itself
Around clouds

Promising us
Tomorrow

Yours

He leaves Hickies
On my heart
A cold spoon couldn't touch
And the taste of whisky on my lips

To remind me
Of whom I belong to

Once

No one
Leaves my heart
Without a stain
That
They've been there...

I'm Gone

He lost me when I discovered myself
Stretched across the world
With
My mind set on utopia
Embracing it all

Cause freedom
Taste like
Cinnamon

Grandfather

He wasn't the same man I once knew
His eyes is what gave him away
And when I spoke, I introduced myself
Hoping his love knew my name

There's only one hope for the sick and the weak
And those things we tend to forget
No matter how old, no matter how bad
Letting go is always—not yet

For now
I choose to soothe my mind
With the thought of his pain being gone
And the strength that I have to write this poem
Is the strength I must have to move on.

In loving Memory of my Grandfather Wallace Gans
March 31st 1927 -December 16th 2003

Rotting

Selfish flesh with elbows to table
Pulling all of me into its arms
Forsaking Gods perfect Laws
Creating distance between its casualty and paradise
Selfish flesh for summoning tasty men
Tasty romance
A full belly as I pick my teeth
Of its sin at dawn

Oh flesh
How you ruin me
How you make me drown
In your offerings

I shall keep praying to rebuke you
Refuse you
In
Me…

Votre amour est comme un bonbon

So sugary daddy
Let this Creole girl experience you
If only
For a short while

My Pierre
Rousing my feminine places
An expert at moan
Manipulation

He takes full advantage
And I
Submit like a good girl should

Incredibly smitten
Encased in his flame

Jamais
Oublie'

Untitled

Music
And War
Just pieces of America
In a gumbo pot

Fist and Afros reaching for the sky
I'd rather do time
In a soul train line

Lord have mercy on us all
Peace is now
Uproar
And freedom smells like
Burning buildings

Politics are weapons formed against us

Like hot sauce on chitlin's
An acquired taste...

Rather sit here and drink this hot coffee
Writing a long list of who to pray for

Cause we aint never known chaos like this

Anyway

Untitled

Making love to
Poetry
Lipstick stains on its
Pages

A word to
Remember
A thought to
Pay homage

I surely know this love
Too well

Untitled

The filth of Money
Shines off in the distance
As we crown vanity
With the love stolen from
God
How great is the death
For a man with grandiose philosophies
Buried alive
With a fist full
Of currency

Untitled

I found myself
With its back to me
Standing on a cliff
In motion to jump

Boy am I glad
I caught it just in time

To tell myself
I love you

Untitled

I'd rather wake up
To your sleepy face
Covered by the morning sun

Then to fall asleep naked
With our backs to one another
Angry at the thought
Of how love
Use
To feel

Untitled

Pickin through my kidney beans
Hair swollen pushed in a knot
Marvin can't keep his words off me
Bellowing tunes with
Echo
The echo creeps through my neighbors
Windows with scent and
Sound

And blackness

Hot water cornbread
Thick as my thighs
Nutty as my color
But
Aint ready yet

So, I wipe my hands on my apron
and chauffer my darling Baby to my hip
To peek at the rice
To make a memory
of my love
My food

My blackness

Untitled

From a distance
He is blandly apart of the element
The busy noise of strangers
Attending to their inquires

He is also a stranger
Just a beautiful smile
Walking quickly away
A mystery
A flavor unknown to my palate

He becomes my ink
My paper
And the first sentence

In my diary...

Random sweet nothings...

We temporarily
stop writing poetry
when we are off somewhere
living it...

A letter to an absent father:
I exhausted my heart with old hatred for you
Now
 I just pretend
You are dead

Vision is not literal sight
It has never been that
Vision is the driving force
Behind the little girl in the ghetto who becomes Oprah

Its simple when you think about it
If I'm to love you
I'm also to forgive you
Love for all the intentional things
Forgiveness for all the human things
But yes love

Nevertheless

The clock should not define the reality of your dreams
And nothing should dictate how far you'll go
Or how long the ride is
Or how beautiful the journey will be.

Printed in the United States
By Bookmasters